Seventeen Letters of Faith, Hope & Inspiration

By: Joseph Tait Miller

The letters were written in this order with a purpose. They build on each other and ultimately culminate with the final message. I would ask that the first time that you read these letters that you start from the beginning. Thank you so much for reading my letters to you!

Letter #1 Bound By Our Decisions

Letter #2 The Goose and The Egg

Letter #3 The Cave

Letter #4 Stars on the Ceiling

Letter #5 The Four

Letter #6 Mosquito Repellent

Letter #7 The Bull Elk

Letter #8 The Basketball Game

Letter #9 The Lord Looketh on the Heart

Letter #10 The Kick

Letter #11 Electric Fences

Letter #12 The Rattlesnake

Letter #13 He Knows Us

Letter #14 The Home From Whence Our Journey Began

Letter #15 Green Beans

Letter #16 Losing Daxton

Letter #17 Endure to the End Zone

Poem: The Reason Why

Bound By Our Decisions

My Dear Friend,

I am so very excited to be able to write these letters to you. I hope that they find you well and that they will in some way enrich your life and brighten your day!

So much of this life passes us by so quickly, that we often fail to see the greater meaning in the day to day events. When we look back at the great minds and philosophers of many generations, I would venture to say that there was much more there than just brilliant minds. These were minds that were willing to take time to ponder and think about the meaning of things that occur in our lives, and the lessons that can be garnered from those experiences.

I will admit this is not always easy to do, but I hope that as you read and allow me to share a few examples from my own life, that you will start to see the relevance and the principles that you and I can learn from them. Once you start, you will find yourself on a journey, and hopefully, you will begin to find greater meaning in the events that we consider to be menial or day-to-day.

My father has always had a passion for plants and farming. In college, he studied plant science and started his working career in that field where he sold seed and fertilizer. He enjoyed working with and advising the farmers that sought his help. When I was about five years old, the company with which he was employed began to move in a different direction, leaving my father with some difficult decisions to be made. Having had grown up with dairy cattle and working a part time job in high school on a local dairy, he decided to venture into the dairy industry. This decision would forever change not only his life, but my life also. The events that constitute my youth and the lessons learned having grown up on the dairy, influence me still today.

When I was about five or six years old, my younger brother Travis and I had the responsibility of feeding young calves, heifers and milk cows while my dad milked. One day, either after finishing our chores, or maybe even in the middle of doing them, Travis and I got the idea that we were going to ride some of the dairy heifers. These heifers were probably about a year old and weighed around 800 pounds. Travis was less than a year younger than myself and was usually the test pilot for most of our crazy ides.

Somehow, it made sense to our five and six year old minds that if we tied a string (a piece of baling twine) onto the foot of the cow, while having the other end tied around the foot of Travis, he would be able to successfully ride the cow without getting bucked off. So, that is what we did. Once the string was attached to Travis, we eased up behind the line of heifers that were calmly eating their hay and managed to get a slipknot loop around one of their legs.

Almost instantly, the lassoed heifer took off running around the corral. She was in a panic, as she now had some foreign object on her leg and a screaming little boy being constantly dragged in her direction as she ran. I too began to panic. I ran from the heifer pen to our house screaming that Travis was dying. I can only imagine the dread that overcame my mother, as this was not the first nor last time that such screams for help would come ringing in her ears. She quickly came out and helped cut Travis loose.

My Friend, on the surface, this is just a silly story of boys being boys. As I now look back at this experience, it dawns on me that there is so much more meaning there. You and I, each in the spheres of our own lives, are constantly having to make decisions. Each of these decisions, even when they might seem small and insignificant, are either binding us more fully to our Savior Jesus Christ, who seeks to lift us up and strengthen us, or binding us to he who would want nothing more than to drag us down into misery and despair. We had made a decision that day as kids, that in a very real sense left Travis bound to the consequences of our actions and bound to being dragged all across that corral.

Our life is a raft that is adrift in a current of water. There is no being neutral. Neutrality does not keep us from going in any direction, but rather allows us to drift out of control downstream rather than upstream, to the destination to which we hope to arrive.

I know that you and I have many challenges that are the same, but I also know that we each have to make decisions in our day-to-day life that are specific to each of us individually. Please try to think about those two little boys, the string and the 800 pound heifer, as you make some of your decisions this week. Is the decision that you are planning to make going to bind you to happiness and move you forward, or take you in an undesired direction?

I hope that you have a wonderful rest of your week! I will write again soon!

Your Friend,

The Writer of Letters

The Goose and The Egg

My Dear Friend:

What a joy it was to hear that you received my first letter! I hope that you were able to relate that silly story of being bound to a cow, to the binding decisions that we make each and every day. I also hope that this letter again finds you well; and, in the event that you are feeling a little down when you read this, I sincerely hope that this letter will help to lift your spirit.

Earlier today, I saw a flock of Canadian Geese fly overhead. It has always fascinated me in a way to watch them fly in a "V" shaped pattern, each taking turns as lead goose. By doing so, they share the burden of breaking the wind in the sky and ease each others difficult burden of traveling. In many ways, you and I do that for one another. Our friendship, our friendships with others, and the loving bonds of family all create an effort of teamwork that helps each of us to continue to fight the fight.

The geese also made me think back to an event of my youth that I wanted to share with you. Ironically, this story takes place just in front of the heifer corral that I described in my last letter. You see, there was a small canal of irrigation water that ran past our little dairy. One day, a domestic goose showed up out of that canal and took up residence in the corrals with the cows. This goose was not a friendly goose. If you were to get too close, it would charge and make a hissing sound that let you know it was not bluffing. This combined with the fact that my father had told me that a goose could flap its wings hard enough to break a kids arm, was more than enough to convince me to keep my distance.

One day this goose did something extraordinary and caught my curiosity completely. Directly in front of the feed bunk, where the 800 pound heifers ate, this goose plopped down onto a nest. Once it started sitting on this nest, it never left. It was there all the time. I wanted so badly to see the eggs that were on the nest, but that goose would not let me even get close. Just feeding the heifers nearby, felt as though I was risking my life.

This carried on for a couple of weeks, until one afternoon as I came around the corner of the corral, I noticed that the goose was gone. After making sure that it was nowhere around and not going to come charging after me, I approached the nest with great excitement, imagining the treasure of eggs that I was surely going to find. To my surprise though, I arrived at the nest and found nothing other than a bunch of down feathers and one single white rock. She had been sitting that entire time on a rock! A rock that to her, must have resembled an egg enough to convince her to build a nest around it.

I could not believe it! She really had spent weeks incubating this rock. The problem was, it was a rock and not an egg. She could have sat on it for all of eternity, and the result would have been the same. She was sitting on an egg that never would and never could hatch. As I look back now, the lesson she taught me is of more worth to me and my life than I could have ever imagined then.

Everyday that we are alive, we are each allotted 24 hours to do with as we will. There are very few things that every single one of us has in common, but time is one of those things. What we do with that time is of great worth. Many of us, myself included, sometimes invest our time and energy in things that are not necessarily bad, but that are not necessarily the best use of our time either. Those things are not all that much different than the goose sitting on that egg. She was sitting on an egg for weeks that would never hatch. There are things in all of our lives that will never hatch into the happiness that we seek to find. They cannot, because in most instances, the nature of those things are of such that they are only there to distract and not bring lasting joy and fulfillment.

I think it is interesting that Jesus taught in John chapter 9, verse 4 that: "I must work the works of him that sent me, while it is day: the night cometh, when no man can work."

He understood the importance to make the most of the time that He had. My Friend, I truly hope this little story in this letter can be of some inspiration today and all of this week for you! I know that you have an uphill battle, as we all do, but that I am here cheering you on! Press forward, and I will write again soon!

Your Friend,

The Writer of Letters

The Cave

My Dear Friend:

I am so very happy to be writing to you once again! It is hard to believe sometimes how fast time goes by and how quickly our lives continue onward. Were you able to identify some of the "eggs that will never hatch" from the last letter? I hope that you were, and that maybe in doing so you have been able to discover other things to put in their place, which will bring even more fulfillment and happiness to your life!

I was thinking today about another experience from my youth that taught me a great lesson on life. You see, there is a cave near where I live that many people do not know about. It is not near any main highway and is tucked away on a seldom traveled dirt road. This cave was made from an air pocket in a lava flow many years earlier and can only be explored on hands and knees, with an occasional opportunity of walking half crouched.

When I was in my mid to late teens I, along with several friends and my brother, decided to stop by this cave while we were out driving and exploring our Idaho desert. We had never initially planned on visiting the cave, but because our travels took us nearby, we decided to go in. Since we did not plan to explore the cave, we entered having only one flashlight between the five of us. In hindsight, that was not the smartest of ideas, as this cave is a tunnel that goes well under the ground for a significant distance.

I need to tell you that this cave is a very dark cave. Once you have crawled in and passed through a couple of chambers, there is absolutely no light. It is the darkest darkness that you can imagine. I am always in awe of how dark it is, and even now, when I visit the cave, I cannot help but turn out my lights to marvel at just how dark it really is. You can place your hand right next to your face and you cannot see it.

We crawled to what would be about the half-way point, as far as the depth of the cave, with our one flashlight. The other guys that I was with, wanted to continue and travel all the way to the back of the cave. I had been there many times before and decided to let them all go on ahead while I waited behind for them to return. I watched them, or rather, I watched their silhouettes crawl along and disappear into the darkness. I was now all alone, and the cave was very dark.

After a short time, I decided it would be funny to crawl to another part of the cave and try to scare the other guys when they returned. I knew it would worry them to find that I was not in the spot where they had left me. I began to crawl, but the elevation of the ceiling of the cave changed constantly. I crawled a short distance and hit my head on the sharp lunar-looking ceiling. It hurt a lot! I wanted so badly to scare the other guys though, so I got myself down into a belly crawl and continued further. It was not long before I hit my head again, and the pain this time was doubled.

I then decided that maybe this was not worth it. As I sat there in the darkness, it dawned on me, that now that I had moved, I could no longer discern in which direction the guys had gone. Everything was so black that I didn't even know which way was out of the cave. It was an eerie feeling. A feeling that I am sure could create a great deal of panic in someone who was claustrophobic. I am not too bothered by enclosed spaces, but that immense darkness and having no light caused some fear within me.

Luckily, a few minutes later I was able to make out light coming from a corner of that vast darkness, followed by silhouettes and cheerful voices. When we were together again, we ventured on and out of the cave. I am so glad that our one single flashlight did not fail us on our adventure. It would not have been easy to find our way without it.

Over time though, I have come to realize that there is an

even greater lesson to be learned from that experience. The reason that I struggled to navigate that cave and had to have more than one encounter with my head crashing into the rock ceiling was because I did not have my own light. We did have light, but it was light that had to be shared, and when our travels took us in different directions, I was left alone in the dark.

It made me think of the parable of the ten virgins and the bridegroom. Five were wise and carried with them oil, and five were not and carried no extra oil. When the time came, that they needed to be found prepared with their lamps lit, their oil was gone and there was none to be shared. We too cannot always rely on shared light. Yes, the light that many great people that we surround ourselves with, can be a great strength to us and help us in the journey of our life a great deal, but without a doubt, you and I, and everyone else that will live in this world will have days of darkness. Days in which we will not be able to rely on borrowed light.

Each of us need to add oil to our own lamps daily. We do this through scripture study, prayer, service and so many other things that brighten our way. When you think about it, every day that you and I live, we wake up and enter the cave of life, which is much like the one we ventured into all those years ago. Parts of the cave are semi-lit and natural light gives a glimpse of the course to be traveled. In parts of the journey, friends, family and righteous leaders will be there to share light with us too. Yet, there will be times where we will need our own light; light that cannot be borrowed, to ensure that we make our journey safely.

My Friend, I hope that perhaps this story will help you to realize just how important it is that you carry your own spiritual flashlight and maybe even some extra batteries as you journey through today, tomorrow and throughout all our lives.

I pray for you My Friend, that in some small way, this story will give you some strength and inspiration to continue fighting the good fight! I will write again soon! God Bless!

Your Friend,

The Writer of Letters

Stars on the Ceiling

My Dear Friend:

I trust that since I last wrote, you have not ventured into any dark caves without the use of a good flashlight. Maybe you carried an extra just in case? Has anything changed in your day-to-day life to help ensure that you will have a greater amount of light available to you? I sincerely hope so!

I want to write to you again and share another experience that has taught me a great deal about light. In the Bible we read in John 8:12, "Then spake Jesus again unto them, saying, I am the light of the world: he that followeth me shall not walk in darkness, but shall have the light of life." That verse has great significance when we compare our lives to the dark cave that I described in my last letter. I want to focus on the light that is shared by others. While there will certainly come moments in our lives where we will not be able to survive on borrowed light, the light that others share with us, and the light that we can share with others, is real and can be very powerful.

In Matthew 5:14-16, The Savior teaches: "Ye are the light of the world. A city that is set on a hill cannot be hid. Neither do men light a candle, and put it under a bushel, but on a candlestick; and it giveth light unto all that are in the house. Let your light so shine before men, that they may see your good works, and glorify your Father which is in heaven."

Here we see that we are to be lights also. I have for many years been intrigued with the example of ships lost at sea, trying to find their way home and back to shore. In the dark, one of the greatest tools that a ship trying to reach harbor has, is that of a lighthouse. We have all seen, or at least have seen pictures, which helps us to imagine and understand the concept of this light-giving tower. One aspect of its functionality that is often overlooked, is that many times other lights, often referred to as range lights or lower lights, are needed to help the ship make the right approach to the land; thus avoiding being torn to pieces in the rocks and coral reefs that are often found near the shore.

These range lights sit much lower than the lighthouse and are often not as bright. Their purpose is to give the traveler a little light to see what is immediately in front of them as they approach, and to give a second reference point as to how to approach the shore. When the sailor is able to line both points of reference together, causing both the range light and the lighthouse to appear as one, they then know that they are on a safe course.

The brighter lighthouse that sits up on the hill I feel represents the Savior in many ways. The range lights or lower lights represent each of us. When we strive to have light, we can become instruments in the Lord's hands to help others to come unto Him.

A few years back, when my oldest son was just a baby, we placed several small, glow- in-the-dark stars on the ceiling in his bedroom. When we would turn out the lights and sing him a song before bed, the stars would let off a glow that was magical. One night, as we went through our bedtime routine, the significance of those stars struck me in a powerful way. I found myself thinking about how those stars worked.

The stars gave off light, but in order to do so, **they first had to come into contact with light themselves**. It was such a powerful piece of insight. The light that they emitted in the darkness truly was magical, yet it was not something that they could produce of themselves. When exposed to light for a period, they became empowered to then also give off light themselves. Unless the exposure to light is repeated, the stars would slowly dim, and the light would go away.

My Friend, for us to be the light of the world that our Savior Jesus Christ desires us to be, we must, like those stars, come into contact with light ourselves. We must be willing to learn of Him, to follow Him, and truly come to know Him -- not just know of Him. When we do that, there will be light in our lives, not just for us, but for our families, our friends, and every other person that God puts in our path. Still, the procuring of light is not a singular event, but rather a daily process that recharges our capacity to share.

My Friend, I hope that you can continue to seek to obtain and retain more of that light. The more light that surrounds all of us will, in turn, make the path that we all must follow easier. I hope these thoughts will bolster and lift you over the course of the next little while, until I write to you again. My prayers are ever with you!

Your Friend,

The Writer of Letters

The Four

My Dear Friend:

I hope this letter comes to you on as beautiful a day as I am having here. The sun is shining, and spring seems to be arriving. The land seems to be changing from the grayish tan color that it carries through the winter to shades of green. I live in an area where many Angus calves are being born, and these little playful black calves seem to be appearing everywhere I look!

Did you go out and buy a small packet of those glow-in-the-dark stars after my last letter? If you didn't, it is never too late. I think that a few on your ceiling would remind you of our correspondence and help remind you of the need to come into contact daily with light! As I have thought about the light that we share with others, another lesson I have learned came to my mind, and I really want to share it with you.

A few years back, I was asked to teach an early morning Bible study class to high-school-age kids in my community. It was a very special experience for me. On one particular day, we were studying in the second chapter of the book of Mark. When you have a moment, please go back and read it. In this chapter, The Savior is teaching in a house in Capernaum, and the multitude that gathered to hear Him teach was so great, that there was neither any more room in the house, nor in hearing distance outside of the door.

It was at this time that a man was brought unto the Savior who was stricken with palsy. When those that brought him arrived, they found that it was impossible to carry the man through all the people unto the Savior. They were persistent and lifted him up onto the roof of the house, where they toiled to uncover the roof and then lower this man down to the Savior. We kind of know the story from there. Jesus not only healed the man of the palsy, but first forgave him of any and all sins that had been a part of his past.

As we studied this, and watched a short video segment depicting the event, something else caught my attention and touched my heart so deeply, that even now as I begin to describe it to you, my eyes swell up with tears. You see, verse three of Mark chapter 2 reads: "And they come unto him, bringing one sick of the palsy, **which was borne of four.**"

So often, I had read that line and did not pay much attention to this phrase describing those that brought the sick man. You see, there were four of them. They were four friends, four family members, four people that cared enough about this man to not only carry him to the place where the Savior could be found, but then also toiled a great deal to actually place him at the Savior's feet. This man, their friend, could not get to Jesus by himself, because of the palsy with which he was stricken.

I have thought about that a lot since. Just as the physical palsy kept this man from being able to come unto the Savior for himself, there exists many forms of spiritual palsy that keeps us and others that we know and love, from being able to come unto the Savior for themselves. That palsy exists in many forms, including fear, embarrassment, pride and others. Those forms of palsy can be every bit as real to those experiencing it, as was the physical palsy that held this man captive. Had it not been for the faith, prayers, and efforts of these four individuals, this man might not have experienced the healing that he experienced -- at least not at that time.

Another thing that struck me was what verse five says, "When Jesus saw their faith..." It was not the faith of the man who was ill, but the faith of the four who brought him that is mentioned here. The test of this life is so specifically tailored to test each of us so fully, that I think that there are times where we each find ourselves in both the position of the four *and* the position of the man with palsy. We all have times where we not only need to extend our hands to help another, but other moments when *we* need that hand extended unto ourselves.

It is so important that we never underestimate our ability to help another. We also must realize that we need not be alone in extending that help. One individual would not have been able to get this man to the Savior. It took the efforts of all four. My Friend, if you will allow me, I would like to take the liberty to describe to you what else I strongly believe happened in that moment. I can see it so clearly in my mind, and feel it burn so deeply in my heart, that I am quite certain it is true.

I believe these four shed tears as they watched this individual that they loved, be healed of his malady. I also believe there was a great likelihood that they themselves, just like you and I, were facing challenges in their own lives that were quite possibly not visible to those around them. I believe that after healing their friend, The Savior looked up at them, looking them each in the eyes with a love and compassion towards them that we can scarcely imagine. In that moment, as they served another, The Savior in His great mercy was also healing them. Though it is not described, those four walked home that day healed just as fully as was their friend. I know this to be true.

These impressions so deeply impacted me, that I wrote a short poem that I want to share with you. I titled it, "The Four."

The Four

There are four of whom ye scarcely know,
Whose love and faith no roosters crow.
For they did not serve for sight nor gain.
But to bless a friend in hurt and pain.

They carried him from oh so far.
To Him whose relation to God was known as "Bar"
To the Son of God, as some proclaimed.

Whose healing power was so well famed.

And yet in arrive found the room full to fill,
No path to carry unto Him this ill.
But rather than turn back or wait at the door,
These four knew that they could do a little more.

They lifted, toiled, how they tried.
Then slats of roof they peeled and pried.
And lowered down this man, their friend
To Him whose power they knew could mend.

They listened as this, their friend was healed.
From both the palsy and sin concealed.
And watched this friend take life anew
Their own understanding greatly grew.

If they yet were here, I'm sure they'd tell
How in blissful peace, their hearts did swell.
His upward gaze pierced their inner soul,
And they four too again made whole.

No one took notice as they walked away.
No Scroll spoke of them the following day.
Yet for the sake of keeping score,
Earth's greatest souls ought include these four.

By: Joseph Tait Miller

My Dear Friend, I doubt many others took notice of the four that helped to bring about this magnificent event. Though they did not seek it, the reward of having the peace instilled in them as 'The Savior of the world' looked into their eyes, was beyond any recompense that they could ever have received. At times we might feel the same way; but I promise you that as you and I strive to lift and bless the lives of others, we will find that we, ourselves, are healed of our own struggles and difficulties.

I hope in some small way that sharing these impressions with you will give you added strength as you continue forward. I pray for you always!

Your Friend,

The Writer of Letters

Mosquito Repellent

My Dear Friend:

I have been very anxious to write to you again. I have another memory and lesson that has been on my mind a lot lately that I really want to share with you. I hope that you too will be able to relate to it in some way.

Have you ever noticed that sometimes we suffer without having to suffer, because we fail to take advantage of the things that we already have around us? Suffering and difficulty of which we had every tool available to help us quickly overcome, but that we neglected to put to use? This happened to my brother Travis and I a few years back.

Growing up in the northwestern part of the United States, we had in front of us an abundance of outdoor activities. One of my favorites has always been fishing for trout. My brother and I ventured a couple hours north of our home to try one of our favorite fishing holes. We arrived and began to fish. Within only seconds we had our first trout on the other end of the line. It was only the beginning to what was going to turn out to be a great afternoon of fishing.

The only problem was that the mosquitoes in this area were absolutely horrible. There was nothing we could do to stop them from biting us, and it was impossible to swat every mosquito that landed on us. We endured this for several hours because the fishing was so amazing. After donating what felt like a gallon of our blood to these little vampires, I blurted out how I wished that we would have thought to bring along some mosquito repellent.

The sudden glance of remembrance that came across my brother's face will stick with me forever. He looked up, almost embarrassed, and said that he thought he might actually have some repellent under the seat of his pickup. Sure enough, we checked and there it was. We applied it to each other in great mists and we spent the last ten minutes of our four-hour fishing trip mosquito free!

It is oddly funny to think about in hindsight, but in the moment, the joys that we were experiencing while catching these great fish, and enjoying one another's company in such a beautiful environment, were somewhat diminished as we suffered through mosquito bites that were not necessary. Though there are many difficulties and trials that come to us in life that we cannot avoid, I would venture to say that in all of our lives, there are also a considerable number of difficulties that could either be avoided or at least more easily overcome, if only we were to use the tools that the Lord has already given us.

I am certain that in my own life, one day I will look back at my performance during this earthly test and see with great clarity those many instances where, if I had only knelt down in prayer, or only sought out answers in the scriptures, or turned to a trusted leader, family member or friend; I would have been able to suffer less and experience even more of the joy that the Lord desires for us during our mortal life. I cannot help but think about the many times in the book of Isaiah where he says, speaking of the Lord, "...but his hand is stretched out still." (Isaiah 5:25, 9:12, 17, 21, 10:4)

I promise you, My Dear Friend, that His hand is stretched out still. It does not matter where we have been nor what we have done, his love for us truly is infinite. He wants us to have joy. He is the truth, "...and the truth shall make you free." (John 8:32)

I continue to pray for you always, My Friend! Be sure to remove the spiritual mosquito repellent from under your seat! I will write to you again soon! God Bless!

Your Friend, The Writer of Letters

The Bull Elk

My Dear Friend:

Due to the nature of my full-time job, working in agriculture, I do not make it into town very often. Today, however, I was in town with a couple of my sons. I could not help but notice in the sporting goods section that there was no mosquito repellent on the shelf. It made me think of you, and I humorously wondered if you had been to my local sporting goods center buying all the repellent after reading my last letter or, if we are just too early in the spring for them to be trying to sell it!

I wanted to write you again and share an encounter that I had with a bull elk in the mountains a few years back. There are very few days that have gone by since, where I have not thought back to the lesson that this bull elk taught me.

I was in the mountains of central Idaho, archery hunting with my good friend, Tyson, from Switzerland. It was about mid-afternoon when we spotted a herd of elk coming off a high mountain, a good mile or more away from us. We could see that this herd was being pushed by a good-sized bull, and so we took off in pursuit. After literally running up and down several smaller hills to try to cut this herd off, we came up over one hillside and found the elk just a few hundred yards from us across a small valley, in the timber. While they had the advantage of being in timber, we did not. We were very much exposed on an open hillside and could not close the distance any further without being seen.

I was using a bugle which mimics the sound of another bull elk. Each time I would do this, the bull across the way from us would become quite agitated and start to aggressively thrash the small Aspen trees that were near him with his antlers. The only problem was that without any cover immediately in front of us to conceal our stalk, there was no chance of getting any closer. This herd had no desire to leave the safety of the timber.

Both Tyson and I were quite new to bow hunting for elk at this time, but we had heard many times that it was next to impossible to pull a herd bull away from his herd of cows. We had an idea. If Tyson could go back in the direction from which we came until he was concealed by hills and timber, and then make a big loop out around this herd and come back from behind them in the timber, he might be able to mimic the call of a lost cow and get this bull to go back uphill to find her. After a time of hiking, Tyson was able to do just that, and located himself just a couple hundred yards above the elk.

The elk were now between us, and I continued to rile the bull by convincing him that just across the valley another bull was taunting him and inviting him to come fight. Tyson then began to make the call of a lost cow. I had the most perfect vantage point to watch what would happen unfold. Through my binoculars, I could almost see the thoughts of this bull in his eyes as they widened, and he turned his head to look uphill from where the lost cow calls were now coming. He stood still only for a few seconds, listened to my taunting bugle one more time, and then began to run uphill to find this other cow.

I have contemplated the response of this bull more than I have ever thought about any other single event in my life. This bull, by standards of things which would make a bull elk happy, had everything in the world. Yet, in a moment of weakness, chose to leave all that was real behind, in pursuit of a mimicked call -- an idea of something more, which was counterfeit. **In essence, he left all that was real behind in pursuit of something which was not!**

I can assure you that no bull elk were harmed in the making of this story! This bull elk ran within yards of Tyson but stopped in a patch of Aspen trees, denying Tyson a lane through which to send an arrow. After a few minutes of not being able to find the cow, he ran back downhill to his herd. Tyson called out again, and again the bull ran to him, but again managed to not provide the right shot through the timber. This time, after not finding what he went looking for, he took his herd and moved on down the valley and away from us.

The lesson, though, was never to be forgotten. As I watched it all unfold, I applied human thoughts and reasoning to his actions. In many regards, we each are prone to the same deceptions that could have easily cost that bull his life. Satan truly is our adversary, and his ability to mimic true and everlasting happiness is quite superb. He wants us to leave behind all that is real, in pursuit of empty promises and momentary pleasure. If he is successful, we can be robbed, or rather **we rob ourselves of those things that are real and that are truly everlasting**.

My Dear Friend, I invite you to look at your own life, and the things that most strongly pull for your attention. Our greatest joy comes from the things that truly are real -- our family and our faith being of most importance! Don't let an imitation deprive you of that joy. I pray that you might be able to look at yourself through the vantage point that I had sitting high above that elk. As you do so, I hope that you can find the strength to more fully identify and commit to that which is real and give no heed to that which is not.

My prayers are with you always. Though the obstacles that face us are not always the same, we seek to travel the same path and arrive at the same destination. I pray that I can in some way aid you. I know that my writing these letters to you is of great aid to me. God Bless You My Dear Friend!

Your Friend,

The Writer of Letters

The Basketball Game

My Dear Friend:

Have you ever wondered if God cares about the things that are important to you? I think that sometimes each of us has moments in our lives where there is something that is of great importance to us, but that we feel foolish speaking about in prayer with our Heavenly Father because we feel it has little importance in the eternities that are before us. Although I believe God wants us to learn to recognize those things that truly are important and those that are not, I believe that being the loving Father that He is, He does care about all things that we identify as being important to us.

Let me share a few insights. First, in the Sermon on the Mount as described in Matthew chapter 7, The Savior teaches of our Heavenly Father in verses nine through eleven saying, "Or what man is there of you, whom if his son ask bread, will give him a stone? Or if he ask a fish, will give him a serpent? If ye then, being evil, know how to give good gifts unto your children, how much more shall your Father which is in heaven give good things to them that ask him?"

God, Our Father, desires to bless us. He desires that we be willing to seek and ask for those blessings through humble prayer. Though he will not grant unto us blessings that are wrong, he desires to bless us with the righteous, sincere desires of our hearts. I know that there are times where we may feel that those prayers go unanswered; and those moments can be some of the hardest to cope with, because we sometimes plead with the most righteous of intentions, and yet the outcome sometimes is left to His understanding and will, not ours. I know, because I offered such prayers and pleadings when we lost our first son. I will share more with you about that in another letter, My Friend. I do know that apart from those moments where the plan that He has for us and our lives is beyond our ability to comprehend, He wants to grant us that which we righteously desire.

When I was teaching the early morning Bible study class to some of the high school students in my community, we studied verses about the Prophet Elisha in the Old Testament in 2 Kings chapter 6. Early on in this chapter, Elisha takes a group of men to Jordan and instructs them to build a dwelling place. Starting in verse four it reads, "So he went with them. And when they came to Jordan, they cut down wood. But as one was felling a beam, the axe head fell into the water: and he cried, and said, Alas master! For it was borrowed."

I have wondered, why would Our Heavenly Father concern Himself in the slightest regard to a lost ax head? The Supreme Being of our universe must surely have demands of much greater importance. Yet, verse six continues saying, "And the man of God said, Where fell it? And he shewed him the place. And he cut down a stick, and cast it in thither; and the iron did swim." Though in the eternities, the lost ax head was not of extreme importance, it was important to that man who had lost it, and being important to him, it was important to his Heavenly Father.

When I was finished with 4th grade, my family moved from Wendell, Idaho where I had previously lived, to a farm near Eden, Idaho. This caused me to start classes in another school. As I went through Junior High and High School, my new school, Valley, was pitted against Wendell many times in sporting events. We never could beat Wendell, and it was tough because these were my childhood friends. Wendell's athletes were so good that those around my age managed undefeated seasons in football and basketball, with State championship titles to boot!

One night during my Senior year, we traveled to my old hometown to square off in a game of basketball. Wendell, if I remember correctly, had not lost a game going back for a couple of seasons, and especially not on their home court. We took the court to warm up, and I, after warming up for a few minutes, returned to the locker room alone, and did something that I had not done before. I had prayed during sporting contests, don't get me wrong. I always knew that half the guys on the opposing team were praying for the same victory and didn't feel right about asking God to play favorites! I entered the locker room, knelt down, and explained to my Father in Heaven my feelings. I explained to Him that this was just a regular season game. I explained to Him that being such, it had no real consequence as far as the tournaments that would come later in the year. I explained to Him that these were my friends that I was playing against, and then asked Him if it would be alright if I could beat them just once!

I went back out onto the floor. The game began. I pulled up a deep three-point shot just seconds into the game in the face of one of my childhood friends. The shot went in and they did not stop. It felt as if I could have shot from anywhere on the court that night, and the ball was going to go through the net. You have to understand that these games were never even close with Wendell. The talent that they had could not be matched. Yet, quarter-by-quarter we kept the lead and eventually the clock ran out and we were still on top. I had experienced a win that I had desired so badly to have.

We never did beat them again. They continued to be dominant from there on out, but I always knew what nobody else knew. I knew of the conversation that I had that evening in the Wendell visitor locker room with my Father in Heaven, pleading for something that in eternity will mean nothing, but that in that moment meant everything to one of His sons.

My Dear Friend, I share this with you that you too might know that Our Heavenly Father does know us. He loves each of us and He cares about those things that in the spheres of our individual, personal lives, are important to us. I pray that you might be able to search for and gain your own personal witness to that love that He has for you. Knowing that he answered that impossible prayer for me that day has helped me to accept His will more easily when I don't get exactly what I ask for. It has helped me to have confidence; confidence in knowing that if it is important to me, it is important to Him.

Until next time, my prayers are always with you!

Your Friend,

The Writer of Letters

The Lord Looketh on the Heart

My Dear Friend:

I usually write to you in the evenings. Today, I have an opportunity to write to you in the early hours of the morning. The sun is shining through my window, and the warmth it gives is better than any blanket! I hope that wherever you may be, that even just reading this will allow you to imagine and feel such warmth yourself!

I wanted to share with you today another lesson that I learned a few years back that has influenced me a great deal. It has to do with not passing judgment on those around us. The truth is, we can never really know what has gone on in the life of another, and even their outward appearance does not always describe who and what they are on the inside.

Shortly after I graduated from high school, I embarked on a voluntary mission for my church. I was assigned to labor and serve the people of Northern Spain. It was an experience that I will never trade for anything in the world. I love the people that I came to know there. I love their foods. I love the goodness that so many have in their hearts.

I was assigned to be in Northern Spain for the period of two years. With only two weeks left of that two-year mission, I was stationed in the city of Bilbao. Bilbao is a huge city. So different from the rural farming community in which I had grown up. In Spain they have something that they call "medio dia." This is a two-hour block from about two in the afternoon 'til four in the afternoon, where all the shops close and everyone everywhere goes home for lunch and a nap. I wish we had those here!

It did little good for us as missionaries to be out on the streets trying to share our message with people during this time, because no one was anywhere to be found. We typically used this time to get lunch ourselves and to study and improve our Spanish-speaking abilities. On one particular day, shortly after two in the afternoon, my missionary companion and I were walking back to our apartment, down a narrow cobblestone street that cars hardly ever used. As we walked, I had an impression that I should talk to the person behind us.

I looked over my shoulder to see if there was anyone behind us. Remember, it was 'medio dia' and the streets were all but empty. When I looked back, I saw that there was a young woman about our age. First of all, I did not feel very comfortable talking to young women at that point in my life. Secondly, she had more piercings in her face than I had ever before seen. Really, she had piercings all over her ears, eyebrows, nose and lips. I instantly thought to myself that there was no way I was going to turn around and talk to this young lady, and I continued to walk.

The only problem was that the feeling persisted so strongly that I could not disregard it. I stopped, turned around, and seeing that she was carrying a type of cloth bag used for carrying groceries, I offered to help her with her bag. She giggled, and I realized that her bag was empty. For a second, I felt like a complete idiot. Just then, she began to speak to us in English and told us how she was walking and admiring us. She told us that just weeks before, she had been living with a Christian family in Texas. She told us how every morning before school, she had been going to the same early morning Bible/Seminary study class that I would be asked to teach a little later in life.

I was absolutely in shock. I had mistakenly passed judgment on her that was not just. I know that had it been left to my own ability to discern, I would have never stopped and talked to this young woman. The truth was, although my eyes and ability to discern could not immediately see who she was and where her life had taken her, The Lord knew her perfectly.

In the Old Testament, 1 Samuel chapter 16 verse 7 reads, "But the Lord said unto Samuel, Look not on his countenance, or on the height of his stature; because I have refused him: **for the Lord seeth not as man seeth; for man looketh on the outward appearance, but the Lord looketh on the heart.**"

My Dear Friend, I know that we each must judge on a daily basis, and those judgments are often what helps to keep us safe. I also know that there are times such as the one I just described, where we can pass judgment that is not correct. I have learned from this experience that we must always have a prayer in our hearts. We must strive to see others as the Lord sees them. He loves them all, just as much as he loves you and me.

As I have become a father, I understand so much more the love that a father has for his children. If we are all to come to this earth as a test, and have the opportunity to learn and grow, why not send us here in a flash of lightning, or by some other means? It is my belief that family is divinely appointed. As we become parents, we can understand to some small degree, the love that Our Heavenly Father has for each of us.

My Dear Friend, my plea to you over the next little while, is that you pray for the ability to look at others through His eyes. I know that as you do, you will start to notice that you can see others more clearly, that your love for them will grow and, in growing, so will your love for the Lord. My prayers are with you always! God bless you My Dear Friend!

Your Friend,

The Writer of Letters

The Kick

My Dear Friend:

I hope that you are doing wonderful! I hope by now you know that it is with great joy that I write these letters and share my thoughts with you. I can only hope and pray that my sharing them with you can be as much of a help to you as it has been for me as I remember, ponder and share.

Today I wanted to share an example with you about forgiveness. That word is one of the toughest tasks that we are commanded to obey in this life. In Matthew chapter 18, verse 21 Peter asks the Lord, "Lord, how oft shall my brother sin against me, and I forgive him? Till seven times?"

The Lord then answered him in verse 22 saying, "I say not unto thee, Until seven times: but, Until seventy times seven." The Lord was not telling Peter here that after the 490th time that it was okay not to forgive. Rather, he was trying to impress upon his mind that no matter how many times, we are to continue to forgive. In Matthew chapter 5, verse 14, Jesus teaches, "For if ye forgive men their trespasses, your Heavenly Father will also forgive you:"

It is such an interesting concept, because each of us has a desire for the Lord to forgive us of our own faults and weaknesses; but we tend to have a desire to hold onto the errors of others, almost in an attempt to hold them captive by the offenses that they have made. Although it can be extremely difficult, we must learn to let those feelings go. Failing to do so not only nullifies the forgiveness that we ourselves desire, but it becomes a consuming force that can ultimately destroy us and deprive us of joy and happiness.

When I was in high school, I had such a wonderful teacher

who taught our home economics class. Her name was Ms. Brock. I loved Ms. Brock. You would be hard pressed to find a more loving and angelic person in this world. Ms. Brock passed away a few years back, but her goodness will always remain! As a high school aged boy, one thing I loved most about her classes was the opportunity to make food! To be able to make and eat food as a class has got to be one of the coolest things ever. Each year around Christmas, our class would make many batches of all sorts of candies.

We were always taught during the candy-making process to follow directions precisely. In some of the candies, if even a single grain of sugar was added or mixed into the batch at the wrong time, the whole batch would crystallize, and it would be ruined. I think that our ability to forgive can be very much of the same. Failing to forgive, even something small, can be like that tiny, almost unseen grain of sugar. When concealed, and mixed into the batch, it can begin to influence the whole of it, ruining the great result that it could have become.

My Dear Friend, when I was in college, I took an upper-level class on poetry. I have always enjoyed poetry, and though this class ended up being much tougher than I could have ever imagined, I learned a great deal. Many of the words that we studied continue to run through my mind today. There was a poem that we studied called: "A Poison Tree", by William Blake. The poem is a story about revenge, but the opening lines teach what I consider to be eternal truths.

It reads:
"I was angry with my friend:
I told my wrath, my wrath did end.
I was angry with my foe:
I told it not, my wrath did grow."

We can all think of times where someone did us harm, but in which we did forgive them freely. When we did, both the person causing the offense and ourselves were freed from the negative feelings that might have arisen. We can also think of other times, where that forgiveness was withheld. Maybe we can even think of withheld forgiveness that we are holding onto even today. Somehow, by holding onto that, we, in our human state, feel that we are able to hold that person captive by their action. By doing so, we allow that crystal of sugar that does not belong to rob us of the happiness that we might otherwise have.

Another difficulty that we face is the temptation to get even or get revenge. The natural man within us has a powerful tendency to want to retaliate. We become deceived into believing that by somehow inflicting pain on our offender, it will somehow alleviate us of the pain that we have felt.

Let me share another story with you. When I was a freshman or sophomore in high school, I went one weekend to help a neighbor as he tagged and vaccinated his Angus beef calves. The calves were not newborns, and they were not all that little either. I would guess they were a few months old and every bit as big and strong as a high school aged boy. I remember walking up behind a calf in the alley, and the calf, as I approached, not only kicked -- but kicked me hard. My response was to immediately kick the calf. He deserved it right? He kicked me unprovoked. Shouldn't I be allowed to do the same?

In the very moment that I kicked the calf in retaliation, he kicked me a second time, even harder than the first. At the moment I was upset. With the passing of time, I have looked back at that moment with the calf as a great learning moment. The first kick I received happened. It just did. Whether there was a legitimate reason for the calf to kick me or not, did not matter. The second kick I received did not have to happen. It came about due to my response of retaliation.

Many times, events in our lives can be the same. We are all going be the receivers of actions or words from others that will hurt us. The pain that we feel in that moment is real. The decision that we have to be able to make, in that moment, is to be able to accept it, forgive and move on, or to retaliate and bring upon ourselves and others even more unnecessary pain and hard feelings.

My Dear Friend, as hard as it can be, please don't kick back. I promise you that the second kick hurt even more than the first! **Please also do all that you can to forgive.** You not only will be freeing the person that hurt you by doing so, but you will also be freeing yourself! You are a wonderful person, My Dear Friend! Don't you ever doubt that! Until my next letter...

Your Friend,

The Writer of Letters

Electric Fences

My Dear Friend:

I was reading today in the New Testament in the book of 1 Corinthians chapter ten. Verse thirteen in that chapter really struck me. It reads, "There hath no temptation taken you but such as is common to man: but God is faithful, who will not suffer you to be tempted above that ye are able; but will with the temptation also make a way to escape, that ye may be able to bear it."

This verse made me think of two other verses found in Ephesians 6:11&13 which say, "Put on the whole armour of God, that ye may be able to stand against the wiles of the devil. Wherefore take unto you the whole armour of God, that ye may be able to withstand in the evil day, and having done all, to stand."

I do believe that. I do believe that though the temptations and trials that come our way in life are going to test us to the very best of our abilities, that none of those temptations or trials will be beyond what we can withstand; and even if we have fallen, they are not beyond what we can overcome. In Ephesians, it goes on to describe that armor of God as being truth around our loins, righteousness as our breastplate, preparation of the gospel of peace as the shod around our feet. It describes our faith as being a shield, as having a helmet of salvation and the sword of the Spirit. And then tells us to pray always.

We would never go into a physical battle without first arming ourselves with the proper shields and weapons, especially when such protection was made readily available to us. However, sometimes it is easy to forget to arm and protect ourselves spiritually. Sometimes we grow so accustomed to seeing and living with the spiritual war that rages around us daily, that we neglect to make the proper preparations -- yet our spiritual survival and that of our families and friends is dependent on us making such preparations.

The fall after I graduated from high school, I spent weekends helping one of my uncles with picking corn from a large corn patch they had grown. They would pick the corn early on Saturday mornings and then spend the day selling the corn in town. I remember going around that corn patch picking corn, and noticing an electric fence around the perimeter, but only being a few inches off the ground. I remember thinking that it being so low was odd.

I had been around electric fences a great deal in my life. On the farm we often used them in areas where we wanted to graze cattle but did not have the luxury of a larger permanent fence. The fence had a control box that would put a low-level dose of electricity out in a pulsing pattern. If an animal were to touch the fence, a quick pulsating shock would startle the animal away from pushing against the fence line. With one or two experiences with the low-level shock, the animals would learn to not push those boundaries.

The fence in my uncle's cornfield was different though. It was far too low to prevent the animals I was used to from getting away. Plus, there were no cows around, and the corn was not going to run off, so what was up with this little fence? I learned it was there to keep other animals out. You see, the skunks and racoons love to eat sweetcorn just as much as you and I do. During the day, when people were around working in the field, these little corn robbers were nowhere to be found. At night though, without some sort of deterrent, they would come with all their family and friends to feast on the corn.

As I thought about this, it made me think about how hard it must be to keep the lower level weeds and plants from touching this low hanging electric wire. Several times as a kid, I had to use a stick or a machete around the pastures that we were grazing to chop down the weeds that would grow up and touch the electric fence. If the weeds were allowed to touch the fence, the water content of the plant, combined with the fact that it was rooted into the ground, would cause the fence to be grounded out. The electric pulse that normally would keep the fence charged, would lose that charge down the plant and into the ground.

In the case of the corn fence, if enough undergrowth was able to touch the fence, the electric charge would not be there when the skunks and racoons came, and they would be able to pass by with ease. One thing that really struck me about all of this, was the Spanish translation for the word "weed." In Spanish, it is "mala hierba," which means "bad plant" when directly translated back into English. When the bad plants were able to grow up and touch the wire, the wire lost its power. Without power, the treasured corn on the inside of the fence became vulnerable to enemies.

My Dear Friend, many things in our lives can be represented by the corn on the inside of the fence. The treasured corn could be our family or even our own personal testimonies of the Gospel of Jesus Christ. When we allow the bad plants, or harmful influences to touch our lives, our power to protect becomes diminished. Our power to resist temptation is lessened, and we become more prone to losing out on both physical and spiritual blessings that we would have enjoyed otherwise.

My Dear Friend, please strive to keep the spiritual power strong in your electric fence. I know that by doing so, the Lord's promise of not being confronted with a temptation that we cannot overcome will be true. If the "bad plants" are already touching our lives in some way, we can do just as we did as kids and cut them down with machetes and sticks so that they no longer rob us of that spiritual power. I wish you the very best until I write again!

Your Friend,

The Writer of Letters

The Rattlesnake

My Dear Friend:

It is definitely beginning to get warmer here where I live. I am so excited for the longer days and warmer months ahead. The only thing I am not excited for are the rattlesnakes. From where I live, there are sections of sagebrush-covered desert to the north and to the south. My encounters over the years with rattlesnakes on the north side have been relatively few, but on the south side of our farms, the desert is a much different story. I want to share a lesson with you that I learned from one snake in particular.

One of our farms, even now, is notorious for having rattlesnakes. I have had a dog get bitten by a rattlesnake when we lived on this farm. Our neighbors, that live on the next farm down, even went to start their barbeque grill one summer afternoon and found a big rattlesnake up in the barbeque rack.

Today, all three fields that make up this farm are under pivot irrigation systems that walk and irrigate automatically. When I was in high school, that was not the case. During the summer, my brother Travis, a neighbor boy and I would all move the hand-line pipe that was used to irrigate these farms. It was a lot of hard work. One week my brother and our neighbor both headed off to scout camp, leaving me behind to move all the lines myself. Due to the fact that I had so many more lines to move, I did something that I had not done prior while moving pipe. I wrapped a Walkman CD player in a ziplock bag to keep it dry and carried it along with some headphones to be able to listen to music while I worked. (Just saying Walkman CD player makes me feel old!)

Although I was a pretty good kid even as a teenager, there was a degree of rebelliousness that I believe every teenage boy experiences. The music I chose to carry with me that day was of the genre of that time, known as "punk rock," and I tended to have the volume a little on the loud side.

I remember that it was more towards the middle of the day, I had already moved several lines over the previous hours. I was in the middle of the farm and pretty much smack-dab in the middle of that field. I started to have thoughts run through my mind; thoughts that almost were rebuking me for having my music turned up so loud. I started to hear the voices in my mind of church leaders telling me that if I could not hear my own thoughts, how could I ever hear the whisperings of the Spirit?

Unfortunately, I pushed those thoughts and feelings aside and continued to listen to my loud music. I was about halfway finished moving this line of pipe, when I suddenly heard the hissing sound that the line makes when you hook up your last pipe and the whole line pressures up. If you don't know what I mean, when you put the last piece of pipe on the line, that last piece has an end plug. With that piece of pipe in place, the water no longer has an end to run out of, and then forces out all the air in the line and begins to irrigate out of the sprinklers that are now under pressure. When that last pipe is in place, the pressuring noise is that of a loud hiss.

I thought it was odd it was making that sound in the middle of the line. It was loud enough that I could hear it over my music. I continued to take a couple more steps and the noise grew louder. I then stopped, pulled my headphones down, and realized that it was not the hissing of the line, I could hear the rattles of the giant rattlesnake that I was standing directly over. Guilt immediately came over me because I knew that just moments before, thoughts had come into my mind that my music was too loud.

I was close enough to the snake that I dared not even take a step backwards for fear that the movement would make him strike. Luckily, this was one of the first years that I had a cell phone. I pulled it out and called my mother, who was able to bring me a gun. For several minutes as I waited, I was forced to listen to the incessant rattling of the snake and contemplate my lack of taking seriously the impressions that had entered my mind earlier. Fortunately, I was able to walk away from the experience unharmed, but I will never forget the experience.

In the Old Testament, 1 Kings 19:11-12 it reads, "...And, behold, the Lord passed by, and a great and strong wind rent the mountains, and brake in pieces the rocks before the Lord; but the Lord was not in the wind: and after the wind an earthquake; but the Lord was not in the earthquake: And after the earthquake a fire, but the Lord was not in the fire: and after the fire a still small voice."

Usually the Lord doesn't speak to us in a loud voice, it is usually, as described in those verses, "still and quiet." My Dear Friend, I believe that sometimes we drown out the opportunities we have, to hear and recognize those promptings that He is trying to give us. It is not just in audibly loud environments, but in any distraction that so fully holds our attention that we are unable to hear. I also believe that this applies to our prayers too. Sometimes we are in such a hurry that even when we pray, our prayer is more comparable to that of placing a pizza order over the phone. Once the order is placed, we immediately hang up and fall right back into the complexities of our life. I think we all, myself included, need to make our prayers more meaningful, and then also take the time to keep the noises and distractions at bay, and **really listen** to what the Lord has to say.

My Dear Friend, I know that He hears and answers our prayers. I pray, that you might be able to take my experience to heart and strive to live in a way that you can hear Him when He speaks to you. I pray for you always!

Your Friend,

The Writer of Letters

He Knows Us

My Dear Friend:

I hope that this letter finds you doing well! I know that it has not been all that long since I last wrote, but a story has been on my mind that I want to be sure that I share with you. I was reading in the very first chapter in the book of Jeremiah, and the Lord teaches Jeremiah a very important principle of His relationship with each of us. In verses four and five it reads, "Then the word of the Lord came unto me, saying, Before I formed thee in the belly I knew thee; and before thou camest forth out of the womb I sanctified thee, and ordained thee a prophet unto the nations."

The Lord tells Jeremiah that even before he existed in any physical form on this earth, that He knew him, and sanctified and ordained him, for the mission that he would accomplish in this life. Shouldn't that empower us to know that even before coming here, the Lord knew us? He knew our abilities and weaknesses and gave us assignments to accomplish during this life. When we rely on His merits, we cannot fail.

My Grandfather told a story that has made me ponder many times just how well the Lord knows each of us. He grew up in Eastern Idaho near the Snake River. Growing up, one thing that he enjoyed doing was hunting pheasants on their farms and along the river bank. One day he went out in pursuit of a pheasant. He hiked all day and was unable to find a single bird. As the day was growing towards an end, he silently offered a prayer as he walked. In that prayer, he told Heavenly Father that if He would only allow one rooster pheasant to fly, that he would not even shoot it. He was so discouraged from not seeing any, that he just wanted to see one pheasant fly.

Moments after uttering that prayer, he said that a large

rooster pheasant took flight from right under his feet. Untrue to the prayer that he had just uttered, he raised his shotgun, pulled the trigger, and watched as bird and feathers came to the ground just a short distance in front of him. I can only imagine the many thoughts that were running through his head in that moment. He told me that he walked up to where the rooster had fallen, and to his surprise, there was no bird. No bird at all. The cover was not thick, and he was certain that if it had survived and tried to run, that he surely would have seen it, yet he did not.

He told me how he had contemplated that moment many times over the course of his life. Had the Lord made that bird jump, just to prove to him the emptiness of the promise he had just made? I do know that my Grandfather took what he told the Lord in prayer much more serious after that. For me, I believe that the Lord used it as a teaching moment. He knew that my Grandfather, and likely any other hunter in the world making such a promise, would be too weak when faced with that opportunity, to let the bird go.

My Dear Friend, I know that the Lord also knows you. He knows you and I better than we know ourselves. That is the reason it is so important that we seek His guidance and His help in our lives. He will not lead us astray. When we come to know that He does indeed know us, it empowers us with a greater measure of faith. The faith to take the steps forward even when we cannot completely see the path that is before us. My Dear Friend, I will write again soon! God Bless!

Your Friend,

The Writer of Letters

The Home from Whence Our Journey Began

My Dear Friend:

I have been thinking about the verses I shared with you in my last letter, wherein the Lord tells Jeremiah that He knew him even before his mortal life. He told him that even before his life on earth, that he was with Him. Have you ever wondered during this life if it is worth all the effort to strive to live right, so that we can return to live with our God?

I mentioned in one of my earlier letters, that I had served a voluntary service mission for my church as a young adult in Northern Spain. One day towards the end of my two-year mission, I was teaching a lesson. In this lesson, the Spirit taught me so much more than any ears that heard what I was sharing. You see, I was due to return home to Idaho in only another two weeks. I asked the individual that I was teaching if he thought that I might possibly be happy if my plane only took me as far as Argentina and then left me there. Obviously, the answer was no, but I pressed further.

Why would I not be happy with that destination? True, it was Argentina, but it was still America, right? South America, but still America. I need to clarify that I have nothing against Argentina. I love the Argentinian people that I know, and if I ever had the opportunity, I would love to visit Argentina. But, why was it that I could not be happy with that as my return destination?

The words that came into my mind are very sacred to me. It was because, **"It was not the home from whence my journey began."** My journey did not start from Argentina. It was not my home. It was not where my family resided. So what about our spiritual journey? From where did it begin? We started in the presence of Our Heavenly Father, but needed the opportunity to leave our heavenly home, gain bodies, prove ourselves and progress. Just like my mission to Spain, our spiritual journey would not be complete unless we returned to our first home, and the presence of our Heavenly parents.

My Dear Friend, if we were to venture on a journey not knowing where we are trying to go, we are likely to encounter a lot of bumps in the road and the river currents of life will likely take us to places that we might not want to go. However, knowing the destination to which we hope to arrive and then following the map that the Lord provides can and will assure that we find joy in the journey and arrive back to that home from whence our journey began. I pray for you always, My Dear Friend!

Your Friend,

The Writer of Letters

Green Beans

My Dear Friend:

I am so very grateful to be able to write to you again! With the warmer weather approaching, it will not be long now, and I will be able to plant a garden. Though my thumb is not the greenest, I still find something magical about putting seeds into the soil, watching them grow, and then producing a crop that I and my family can consume.

I mentioned to you in the very first letter that I wrote, that my father sold seed and fertilizer during the early years of my life. For this reason, gardening and plants were very much a part of my growing up years. I wanted to share with you something that happened during those years. When I was probably about seven or eight years old, I got my hands on some green bean seeds. I was also very active in the raising of our baby dairy calves at that time, and had access to grain buckets.

Without anyone else noticing, I took one of the grain buckets that we used for the baby calves, filled it with dirt, and planted a handful of green bean seeds in the bucket. I then watered it good, and placed the bucket in a cabinet under the sink inside the muck-room bathroom of our house. This was the place where we had to take our muddy boots and dirty clothes off before entering the rest of the house. No one ever opened that cabinet under the sink, and I knew that it would be warm and safe there while the seeds germinated.

Well, like most kids, my memory of my bean project faded quickly. I completely forgot about the beans for many days. It was likely that a couple weeks passed without me remembering. When I finally remembered, I rushed to my bean stash and opened the cupboard doors. To my surprise, these beans were well approaching a foot tall. I had seen many bean plants before, and this is **not** what they looked like. These plants were all stem, and the leaf system so far away from the roots.

You see, the beans that I had seen before on the farm and in the garden grew until they protruded up and out of the soil and the leaves could receive sunlight. Inside this dark cupboard, even after breaking through the soil surface, there was no sunlight to be found. These beans had thus expended every ounce of energy contained within them to fuel their growth upward, never giving up on their search for light. I have often thought about those beans and how, despite having the trial of being overwhelmed with darkness, they did not ever give up on their search for light.

At another moment, I can remember trying another experiment with bean seeds. On this occasion, I took the seeds and planted them in the ground in all different directions. Some planted on their sides, others pointing up and down. I thought that I might be able to confuse the seeds into not knowing in which direction to grow. I did not think about gravity or the effects of the soil above the seed being warmer than the soil below. I just wanted to see if I could confuse them. I obviously failed in my attempt, as they all grew upward.

My Dear Friend, as you have noticed in my letters to you, I learn a lot from examples. I hope that these examples of the beans never giving up on searching for light, and how no matter the twists and turns that were thrown their direction as they were planted; they always directed their growth upward, can be images that you can also draw strength from. Until my next letter!

Your Friend,

The Writer of Letters

Losing Daxton

My Dear Friend:

As the Christmas season approached in 2009, the life that my wife, Jeanny, and I were living was as good as it possibly could have been. We were both just a couple of semesters from finishing up our college education, we were so happy to be married, so excited for the adventure of life together, and we were expecting our first child, a little boy who we had already named Daxton. We were so very excited to be parents. Although he was not due for a few more weeks, we had everything ready for him.

We sang children-themed gospel songs to him every night, and read scriptures to him, knowing that he could hear us from inside of Jeanny. We traveled to be with my family for the first part of the Christmas break and planned to spend the other half with Jeanny's family. On Christmas Eve, something drastically changed. That evening, we noticed that Daxton was not moving like he always had before. We were concerned but didn't want to get too alarmed. We called the hospital, and they told us to have Jeanny drink cold water and try putting herself in different positions to see if he would start moving. It did not seem to help.

Night wore on to early morning and we went to the hospital. Being Christmas morning, the hospital was quiet. They quickly took us back and a nurse began to check Jeanny. Soon a specialist came in and began an ultrasound, which revealed to us that Daxton's heart was no longer beating, and that he was gone. Never at any moment in my life has the pain and despair taken me so strong as at this moment. I begged and pleaded with God that this not be what was happening. We loved and longed for our dear Daxton so very much.

My sobbing was so intense that my head hurt in a way that I cannot explain. I began to dry heave and shake, and I was at a point that I could almost feel my body and spirit separating. Our world had just completely come crashing down. I cannot begin to describe the feelings that we felt as we started induction and waited for our lifeless baby to be born. Throughout the night, we heard the newborn cries of other babies, knowing that when ours came, there would be no such cries. The following morning, our precious Daxton was born. He was perfect. Doctors found no sign of anything abnormal to explain to us why this had happened.

My Dear Friend, I share a little of this with you because these were some of the darkest days of my life, and yet I know that Jeanny and I were not alone in this. I know that God was with us. I know that He knew perfectly our pain and knew how to comfort us. For both Jeanny and I, the very timing of this event was a 'tender mercy' from God. On the very morning that we were to be celebrating the birth of Our Savior, we were experiencing this great loss. As we commemorated the one person that could make us whole, we were learning of our need to be made whole again.

During the great storm that was on us, there was a peace that could only come from above. I did learn a few other lessons, even after this experience, that will forever change the way I live. Within ten days of all of this happening, I was back in classes at the university where I was studying. While everyone else was full of happiness having just come back from Christmas break, my life and heart were completely broken.

The hardest thing about this for me, was that none of my friends in these classes had any idea what had happened. I did nothing to reveal it either, but it dawned on me that if all these people who were my friends, classmates and instructors knew nothing of what I had just experienced, how likely was it that I had people around me that had major struggles that I could not see either? That has changed me and how I look at others.

The truth is, My Dear Friend, it is likely that everyone

around us is fighting a much bigger battle than we realize. They need our love and support, even when we do not know about their struggles.

I share this too, because your life and mine will yet have many difficulties and challenges. If we keep the Lord close to us, we will be able to overcome them, and we will become stronger as a result. Having suffered to the extent that Jeanny and I suffered made our marriage relationship stronger than anything ever could have. We had nowhere else to really turn to in those darkest hours, except to each other and the Lord. Our love for one another and the Lord grew beyond measure. We have since had four more boys. We could never have imagined that being possible while in those darkest moments, and yet, here we are. Having had this loss, we love our boys so much more than I think we ever could have otherwise.

Over the years, I have thought a lot about the purpose of pain and suffering. I do know that without it, the love and joy that I experience could never have reached the levels that it does now. We truly cannot taste the sweet having never tried the bitter.

There is a story shared by another that runs through my mind often. Elder David A. Bednar of the Quorum of the Twelve Apostles of The Church of Jesus Christ of Latter-day Saints, shared this story from one of his friends. This friend, who was newly married, had purchased a new pickup truck and taken it to the mountains to cut wood. The place that he traveled to was covered with snow, and when he pulled off the road to begin cutting wood, the truck became stuck in the deep white powder.

He was unable to get the truck unstuck, but having no other alternative, he decided to go ahead and cut the wood that he had come for. With time, he filled the entire bed of the truck with wood. Still not knowing what to do, he climbed back into the truck and tried again to free himself from the snow. This time, the weight of the wood in the bed of the pickup was sufficient to give a considerable amount more traction to the truck, allowing it to pull free from the clutches of the snow.

You see, "It was the load" that gave him the traction to be set free. It was the heavy load that gave him traction, allowing him to move forward when he otherwise could not.

My Dear Friend, I know that the tests of this life sometimes feel as if they are more than we can bear. Every one of us will have hours where the darkness feels too immense to escape. Sometimes we may even feel the load that is put upon us is to blame for those feelings. I promise you my Dear Friend, that if you will not give up, if you will continue to push forward and seek and trust in the Lord, you will ultimately find yourself moving forward, with the traction that will set you free from that despair.

You are not alone. You are never alone. Others have experienced the very difficulties that you and I face. More importantly, the Savior knows the difficulties that we face. In John 16:33 He declares, "These things I have spoken unto you, that in me ye might have peace. In the world ye shall have tribulation: but be of good cheer; I have overcome the world."

I continually pray for you My Dear Friend! Remember,**"It was the load."**

Your Friend,

The Writer of Letters

Endure to the End Zone

My Dear Friend:

I have shared a great many things with you over the last little while. I hope that you can feel the love that Our Savior has for you through these letters. I will admit to you, that I have struggled my whole life with the fear of speaking. Yet, I feel that the Lord has helped me to be able to learn these lessons so that they can be shared with others. I fear that in not sharing them, I would be like the servant in the parable of the talents who hid his talent out of fear. I sincerely hope that by writing, I have been able to bless you in some small way. I have one more lesson that I desire to share with you.

A few years back, I was watching a college football game between the University of Oregon and the University of Utah. I do not even know why I ended up watching this game, as I do not follow either team, really. Oregon at the time was one of the top college football teams in the country. As the game got underway, Utah came out with a dominance and resilience that through the opening quarter seemed unmatchable.

Utah lead by a touchdown after that first quarter and had the ball back with momentum, to start the second. The very first play of the quarter was a deep pass that appeared to result in an 80-yard touchdown score. As Utah piled onto their receiver in the end zone, celebrating what appeared to now be a 14-point lead and all the momentum in the world, one of Oregon's defenders who had given pursuit realized that the referee standing at the goal line was still standing there, and had not signaled a touchdown.

This defender, after looking at the referee for a moment, picked up the ball and ran it all the way back the other direction scoring a touchdown for Oregon. When the play was reviewed, video evidence showed that prior to crossing the goal line, the Utah receiver began to celebrate early and had actually dropped the ball at the one-yard line. Now, rather than leading 14 to 0, the score was actually 7 to 7, and the tremendous amount of momentum that Utah had built up to that point was now gone. Oregon went on to win the game.

In both Mark 13:13 and Matthew 24:13 there is record of the Savior teaching, "he that shall endure unto the end, the same shall be saved." After seeing the image of this ball being dropped at the one-yard line, I will forever in my mind see the words "enduring to the '**end zone**' instead.

You see, the prize of a touchdown was not awarded, because the end zone was not reached. By dropping the ball at the one-yard line, all of the effort of taking the pass the length of the field was forfeited. The Savior has taught that we must endure unto the end. As I have watched this re-play over and over, another tremendous truth stands out to me. **It does not matter how well we started, if we do not finish**. Utah came out playing excellent ball, but when they dropped the ball at the one-yard line, the course of the entire game was changed.

Sometimes in life, we are tempted to say or feel, that we have already done enough. It is possible that up until this very moment of our lives, we have done everything that the Lord has asked of us. Yet, just as dropping the ball at the one-yard line forever changed the course of that game; spiritually dropping the ball at the one-yard line can forever change the course of our lives and even our eternities. **My Dear Friend, Endure to the End Zone!**

That said, if you ever do drop that ball, know that the game is not over. Though the course of that game did change and changed drastically, the score was still tied. The game did not end on that play. In fact, there were essentially three quarters yet to be played. We all make mistakes in our lives. That does not mean the game is over. Satan wants us to believe that, but it most certainly is not true. We have the opportunity to change that course. We have the opportunity to change it NOW.

As a kid, I jokingly used to tell other kids that the basketball player Reggie Miller was my cousin. I saw him once do the impossible, of scoring eight points in nine seconds to bring his team from behind to beat the New York Knicks. It seemed impossible, yet it was done. **With the help of Our Savior Jesus Christ, there is nothing impossible.** If we are willing to come unto Him, and allow ourselves to be healed by Him, and then continue faithful unto the end, we will come out on top!

My Dear Friend, it has been a tremendous pleasure to share these insights with you. I have known in my heart for many years that I would one day be writing this. It is liberating, in a sense, to have now written it all down. My heart is full! God Bless You My Dear Friend!

Your Friend Forever,

Joseph Tait Miller
The Writer of Letters

The Reason Why

I there once stood in a mansion fine,
And there was taught that it could all be mine.
But as it was, I could not stay
For I must choose to walk this way.

Thus a plan was laid before my feet
That I with others chose to entreat.
Yet deep inside I did a little fear.
For what if I failed to return here?

Yet in that moment, I felt a hand
For my Elder Brother did near me stand
My fear now gone with a single touch
I loved my Brother, Oh so much.

He promised me He would not fail.
That if I was faithful, I would prevail.
He told me all, what I then must do.
And that He'd be there to help me through.

He said, "The path is narrow and yet it is straight.
This path will lead you to the gate.
And to further show you how much I care,
You will find it is me who is waiting there.

For I do look forward to see your face.
To search your eyes and the embrace.
And then to tell you job well done
To give you glory, the glory of the sun."

I then watched as he went forward, so brave and bold.
To teach the world of a wealth untold.

I watched Him heal, I watched Him bless.
He restored things that were once a mess.

Yet there were many who still denied
And for their sakes I hurt and cried.
For it was not only that they did refuse,
But their own Savior they did abuse.

They hung him on a cross so high,
And for them and me, he there did die.
Then with all glory to His name
He arose my Savior still the same.

I rejoiced for now this thing was sure.
That I then too would rise once more.
And now I too have come to earth.
And entered life through humble birth.

Once again I've come to know His plan
And desire to share it with all of man.
So this I'll do with little rest
For this is when my life's the best.

By: Joseph Tait Miller

Made in the USA
Columbia, SC
14 April 2023